GARDEN~INSPIRED

SILK FLORALS

GARDEN~INSPIRED

SILK FLORALS

{ TERRY L. RYE }

NORTH LIGHT BOOKS

cincinnati, ohio

www.artistsnetwork.com

{ ABOUT THE AUTHOR }

Terry Rye has a passion for flowers and the best job in the world—creating innovative and beautiful floral designs. Since 1980 she has been the owner of The Mariemont Florist in Cincinnati, Ohio. The Mariemont Florist has been featured in the prestigious Cincinnati Flower Show and is listed in the distinguished international directory, Fine Flowers By Phone. As a self-taught floral designer, Terry loves to share the joy of floral arranging with others through her series of floral how-to books and has appeared on the DIY Network, part of the HGTV family. She has also been featured in various trade publications nationally. Terry resides in Cincinnati, Ohio, with her eight-year-old daughter, Sarah.

Garden-Inspired Silk Florals. © 2003 by Terry L. Rye. Manufactured in China. All rights reserved. No part of this book may be reproduced in any form or by any electronic or mechanical means including information storage and retrieval systems without permission in writing from the publisher, except by a reviewer, who may quote brief passages in a review. Published by North Light Books, an imprint of F&W Publications, Inc., 4700 East Galbraith Road, Cincinnati, Ohio 45236. (800) 289-0963. First edition.

Other fine North Light Books are available from your local bookstore, art supply store or direct from the publisher.

06 05 04 03   5 4 3 2 1

Library of Congress Cataloging-in-Publication Data

Rye, Terry L.
    Garden-inspired silk florals / by Terry L. Rye
              p. cm.
    Includes index.
    ISBN 1-58180-282-X (alk. paper)
    1. Silk flower arrangement. I. Title.

    SB449.3.S44 R94 2003
    745.92--dc21
                                    2002027862

editor: Catherine Cochran
designer: Andrea Short
production coordinator: Michelle Ruberg
production artist: Matthew DeRhodes
photographers: Christine Polomsky and Al Parrish
photo stylist: Jan Nickum

metric conversion chart

TO CONVERT	TO	MULTIPLY BY
Inches	Centimeters	2.54
Centimeters	Inches	0.4
Feet	Centimeters	30.5
Centimeters	Feet	0.03
Yards	Meters	0.9
Meters	Yards	1.1
Sq. Inches	Sq. Centimeters	6.45
Sq. Centimeters	Sq. Inches	0.16
Sq. Feet	Sq. Meters	0.09
Sq. Meters	Sq. Feet	10.8
Sq. Yards	Sq. Meters	0.8
Sq. Meters	Sq. Yards	1.2
Pounds	Kilograms	0.45
Kilograms	Pounds	2.2
Ounces	Grams	28.4
Grams	Ounces	0.04

{ DEDICATION }

•

With appreciation, I dedicate this book to my parents, Dot Rye and Walter Rye, for their guidance, support and continuous encouragement throughout my life.

{ ACKNOWLEDGMENTS }

•

Many thanks to all the talented people at The Mariemont Florist for their support and dedication during the completion of this book and for their contributions.

Many thanks to my editor, Catherine Cochran, for her meticulous note-taking throughout the step-by-step process and her creative input in making this a truly garden-inspired floral book. Also, to Christine Polomsky, for her exceptional photography and ability to conceptualize photos that are clear and easy to understand.

I am truly blessed with a talented staff, a great publisher, wonderful friends and an incredibly supportive, loving family. I am thankful for my wonderful daughter, Sarah, who never lets me lose sight of what is important in life … our loved ones.

{ table of contents }

{ introduction }

BRING THE BEAUTY OF NATURAL FLOWERS INDOORS AND CREATE A FRESH AND INVITING DÉCOR WITH GARDEN-INSPIRED SILK FLORALS. SILK FLOWERS HAVE COME A LONG WAY. THEY ARE NO LONGER BORING, MUTED AND LIFELESS. INSTEAD, SILK FLOWERS HAVE BECOME STYLISH AND NATURALISTIC ACCESSORIES IN HOME DÉCOR. TODAY YOU CAN CREATE ARRANGEMENTS USING FLOWERS THAT LOOK LIKE YOU PICKED THEM FROM YOUR GARDEN AND HAD THEM ARRANGED BY A PROFESSIONAL.

As an experienced florist, I meet people who would love to have the look of fresh flowers in their homes, but because they can be expensive or require maintenance, they are looking for an easy and convenient alternative. With silk flowers available in a multitude of colors, textures, sizes and varieties, you can beautifully accent your home with "garden-fresh" silk arrangements.

The projects in this book are divided into four gardens: Romantic Garden, Field Garden, Beautiful Bulb Garden and Fruit & Vegetable Garden. The arrangements featured in the Romantic Garden have a more formal structure, while the projects in the Field Garden are whimsical and loose. The projects featured in the Beautiful Bulb Garden are arranged by groupings and varieties of spring bulb flowers, while the

Fruit & Vegetable Garden projects use realistic faux fruits and vegetables. The beginning of each chapter lists flowers common to the specific type of garden so you can add your own personal touch to these arrangements. You will find arrangements that suit your tastes, from formal to casual, with the seventeen projects shown step-by-step. There is also information and suggestions for varying your arrangement from season to season.

Use this book as a starting point. Customize the projects according to your own personal preferences. You may substitute flower varieties and colors to suit your décor and reflect your own unique style and tastes. Personalize these arrangements and give them as gifts, or fill your own home with the natural beauty of garden-inspired silk florals.

Before you get started on the step-by-step projects, familiarize yourself with the basic tools and floral supplies you will need to successfully create your garden-inspired silk arrangements.

1 Candle Adapters • These are useful when adding candles to a floral arrangement. Insert an adapter into the floral foam.

2 Chenille Stems • Chenille stems are similar to pipe cleaners and are used to secure bows and floral materials. They consist of bendable, twisted, heavy wire and a flocked material that allows water to flow through.

3 Craft Glue • This universal glue can be used as an adhesive for silks and moss.

4 Floral Adhesive • Floral adhesive works on wet and dry surfaces and dries clear.

5 Floral Scent Spray • This spray gives silk arrangements a fresh floral scent. Use it on all of your projects as a final touch.

6 Floral Glaze • Use floral glaze to give dried and silk flowers a protective and glossy finish.

7 Glue Gun • Use a hot glue gun to secure stems or reinforce arrangements.

8 Floral Anchors • These plastic anchors are glued into the containers to secure foam.

9 Floral Spray Paint • This paint is great for enhancing floral containers. It is available in many colors, including metallics, so you can easily create the look of brass or pewter with an ordinary pot.

10 Floral Foam • For the projects in this book, use dry floral foam, which is commonly used with silk and dried flowers. Oasis is a common brand name for floral foam. Both foam sheets and foam bricks are used in this book.

11 Floral Picks • Wooden floral picks come in several sizes and are useful in securing weak stems as well as extending stem lengths.

12 Floral Pins • Use floral pins when necessary for securing moss to floral foam.

13 Floral Tape • Used to wrap stems and secure flowers, bows and wire, floral tape comes in white, brown, light and dark green.

14 Floral Wire • This wire comes in different weights or gauges. It is used to strengthen stems and bind flowers together. All of the projects in this book use 20-gauge wire.

15 Hyacinth Sticks • Available in various lengths, use these wooden sticks to secure bricks of foam and extend stem lengths.

16 Paring Knife • A paring knife is useful for cutting floral foam and tape.

17 Tape Measure • You will need a tape measure to measure stem lengths and the dimensions of the containers.

18 Sand • Sand is an inexpensive way to weigh down lightweight containers such as tin and aluminum.

19 Waterproof Floral Tape • Used to wrap stems and secure containers, this tape comes in white and dark green.

20 Wire Cutters • You need easy-to-handle wire cutters to cut thin-stemmed silk flower stems or dried materials, as well as florist wire. For heavier stems, a stronger pair may be needed.

All of the arrangements in this book were created to look as if you picked the flowers fresh out of your garden and created a natural, realistic arrangement. There are many varieties of flowers to work with, so choose your personal favorites when it comes to color, flower variety and size. While there are basic flower-arranging guidelines, the most important thing is that your creations reflect your personal style.

When choosing flowers to design your own arrangement, decide on the overall theme you want to convey. Do you want a centerpiece that is casual and airy with country flair or do you want something linear and tightly designed for a dramatic accent in a contemporary room? Think about where you want to display the arrangement, the décor of the room, the size and proportion of the arrangement and the mood you want to create. When creating an arrangement in a bedroom, for instance, you may want to use small, pastel flowers for a soft, relaxing mood, while more dramatic and powerful reds and yellows are more appropriate in an active room, like the kitchen or study.

As in the garden, many of the projects in this book include flower varieties that naturally grow well in the same environment, during the same time of year, and therefore would naturally be arranged together. Other projects, such as the Rose Garden centerpiece, focus on one flower variety. No matter if you want to use one or multiple varieties, it is a good idea to create a bouquet in your hands when choosing the flowers. This way you can ensure that the flowers complement each other in color, style and proportion. Don't be afraid to mix and match shades and experiment with new color combinations. For

If you properly care for your silk flowers they will last for many years.

single variety arrangements, combine blossoms with slight color variations to add depth.

When you buy silk flowers, make sure that the flowers are true to life. The color and texture should resemble the flower's natural counterpart. Choose flowers with wired stems and leaves so you can bend them naturally to look realistic. You may also want to use flowers with thick, woody stems for added strength. When purchasing flowers, look for bunches that have a full bloom, a medium-sized bloom and a bud. To achieve the garden-inspired look, buds and various-sized flower blooms enhance the natural look of the overall arrangement.

WAYS TO CUT COSTS

{1}

Use moss to cover floral foam so you don't need as much greenery or flower stems.

{2}

Purchase flowers and greenery at the end of the season to use the following year, when they are on sale.

{3}

Choose cost-effective materials such as decorative sand, marbles, pebbles and crystal chips to fill in glass vases.

{4}

Find containers and vases in thrift stores and flea markets. You can always paint a container for a new look.

{ Caring for Silk Flowers }

☑
Keep silk flowers indoors out of direct sunlight so the colors will not fade.

☑
Use a damp cloth or a hairdryer to clean off the dust on silk flowers every few months. For arrangements in the bathroom, kitchen or on a mantle, you may want to clean them more frequently.

☑
Avoid using water in your silk arrangements. Water may cause the silk dyes to run and bleed.

*T*he container you choose for your arrangement is just as important to the overall presentation as the flowers themselves. It will add to the theme, style and mood of the arrangement. Be creative when searching for containers. You do not need to go out and buy an expensive vase to create an elegant or sophisticated floral arrangement. Check out garage sales and flea markets and update ceramic pots with paint. You can also find unique and distinctive containers of various sizes and colors at discount stores. Remember, while the appearance of the container is very important, it also serves a practical function—it must hold the weight of the arrangement.

Ceramic Containers

Ceramic containers are extremely versatile and usually are sturdy enough to hold the weight of an arrangement. Stylistically, you can use ceramic containers as is, or you can spray paint them with metallic paint to create the look of pewter or brass. They are also excellent for holding trellis and topiary arrangements.

Metal Containers

Tin or galvanized aluminum containers add a country-fresh look to any arrangement, while brass, pewter or polished aluminum create a sophisticated, more formal look. However, these containers can be very lightweight. Fill the base of the container with sand so it can withstand the weight of the flowers.

Glass Containers

From simple to contemporary styles, glass vases are the most versatile and look great in any room. Pay attention to the diameter of the vase opening versus the diameter of the base. With glass containers, the weight and thickness of the glass is the most impor-

The container you choose will add to the overall style of your floral arrangement.

tant. The thicker the vase, the more weight it can hold. In place of floral foam, fill your glass containers with marbles, decorative sand or glass pebbles. For the illusion of water, you can use Lucite, a clear, floral arranging compound that hardens to hold your stems in place. For more directions on using this compound, see page 15.

Unusual Containers

Look around and be creative! There are so many possibilities for unique arrangements. In an arrangement for the kitchen, you may want to use a pitcher, milk jug, watering can or teapot. Instead of a window box, recycle a wooden crate. Use a vintage umbrella stand in the front entryway. Just remember that the flowers and the container should be balanced to work together for the overall desired effect.

$\mathcal{M}$ost of the projects in this book use spring and summer flowers, but there are many ways to keep your arrangements blooming all year long. In order to create realistic-looking arrangements, remember how these flowers behave in nature. Use this section as a guide for displaying seasonally-appropriate arrangements throughout the year.

Spring

Think about what you see when you walk outside on a beautiful spring day. Flowers with small, thin petals are budding and bright colors are all around you. The blooms as well as the foliage are delicate, with soft greenery and bladed grasses. Consider using bulb flowers such as tulips and hyacinths. The choices for springtime flowers are endless, from peach blossoms, blooming branches and forsythia to pansies, which are the first flowers to bud in the spring because they can withstand frost.

Summer

In the summertime, flowers have matured into full blooms. The colors are lush and more intense with open blooms and a heavy petal count. The greenery is a more vibrant green than in the spring. There are few to no buds on stems and flowers have tall, thick stems. Mature, summertime silk flowers are the easiest to find. Consider popular blooms such as peonies, geraniums, lisianthus, larkspur and delphinium, or even bedding plants, like begonias and petunias. For greenery, use ivy to complement your summer bouquets.

Autumn

The beauty of autumn flowers lies in their rich, golden tones. Harvest colors, faded fall leaves and warm, earthy reds, oranges, yellows and jewel tones make exquisite arrangements for Halloween, Thanksgiving, or for everyday use. Add gourds and pumpkins to your arrangements for a festive touch. Use flowers such as cosmos, gerbera daisies, black-eyed susans, statice and yarrow. Incorporate greenery such as bittersweet and corkscrew willow, and add dried materials like wheat for texture.

Winter

While most people associate winter arrangements with evergreen and poinsettias, there is actually a large selection of flowers, berries and greenery available. Winter greenery has hearty stems with larger leaves and heavy foliage. You often find flowers in whites and jewel tones. Metallic silver and shimmering gold accents complement festive holiday arrangements. Winter produces dramatic flowers, such as magnolias, amaryllis, azaleas, cyclamen and paperwhites. Complement these flowers with pepperberry, evergreen, holly, pinecones, birch branches and mistletoe.

{13}

Even if you are a beginner, you can make beautiful garden-inspired arrangements with little or no experience. There are some basic techniques that will help make the process quicker and easier. Keep these pointers in mind as you work on the projects featured in this book.

[cutting stems]

a) Cut at the Notches

All of the projects in this book give specific stem lengths for each flower. Often the stems are thick or made with very durable wire, making them difficult to trim, even with wire cutters. Many stems have notches at various lengths. Cutting the stems at these notches will make the trimming easier.

b) Bend and Snap

For stems without notches, you may have difficulty trimming them to your desired length because of the strength of the wire or the thickness of the stem. In those instances, try the "Bend and Snap" method. This is an excellent method for woody stems or hearty summer and fall stems.

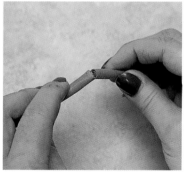

{**I**} *Use your wire cutters and cut as deeply as you can into the stem.*

{**2**} *Bend the stem to weaken the wire.*

{**3**} *As you bend the stem back and forth, it will snap.*

[separate flower stems and foliage]

When you purchase silk flowers, they are often smashed and flat. For a natural-looking arrangement, you must separate the foliage and the petals as well as bend the stems. Watch as these flowers come alive by making simple adjustments.

{1} *Originally, the silk flower is tightly folded up and smashed. Prepare to adjust the foliage, stem and petals.*

{2} *Beginning with the stem and the leaves, slightly bend the tips of the leaves so they point downward. The flower does not have to be completely symmetrical; in fact, it will look more natural if the leaves are not all identical.*

{3} *Open up the flower petals and make any necessary adjustments to the flower so it looks like its natural counterpart.*

{15}

working with Lucite Floral Arranging Compound

Clear Floral Arranging Compound is a liquid compound that hardens and seals the flowers creating a permanent arrangement. Use Lucite floral arranging compound when creating floral arrangements in a glass container to give the illusion of water. The compound hardens after 48 hours to hold the stems in place, solidifying the arrangement. Keep the following tips in mind when working with Lucite, as in the Springtime Vase arrangement on page 44.

{1} *Carefully follow the manufacturer's instructions when mixing the compound. Take necessary precautions and wear latex or rubber gloves.*

{2} *Combine the compound in a pitcher. Trim all stems to the appropriate length and coat them with the compound. Allow each stem to dry before you arrange the piece. If you don't coat your stems, you run the risk of having the dye from your stems bleed into the Lucite, discoloring and ruining the arrangement.*

{3} *Design the arrangement in a separate dry pitcher. Once you have the arrangement the way you want it, transfer it to the Lucite compound container.*

{4} *Once you have added the flowers to the compound, leave it undisturbed for at least 48 hours. If you pick up the vase, you may slosh the compound around, creating a distracting and uneven water line.*

The classic elegance of the flowers grown in a romantic garden inspired the arrangements in this section. Roses, daisies, forsythia and delphinium are just a few of the flowers used to create the timeless beauty in these projects. The flowers

· r o m a n t i c g a r d e n ·

themselves are large and abundant, and the arrangements are structured and formal. The delicate blooms featured are arranged to appear sophisticated and graceful. Display these arrangements in more formal areas such as a dining room or front entryway as a gracious way to welcome guests to your home.

section *1*

popular romantic garden flowers :

DAISY · DELPHINIUM · FORSYTHIA · FREESIA · LARKSPUR · LILAC · LISIANTHUS · MAGNOLIA
PANSY · PEONY · RANUNCULUS · ROSE · SWEET PEA · VIOLET · WISTERIA

rose garden

Roses have long been known for their stately elegance and lasting beauty. This lovely centerpiece is truly a vision from an English garden, touched with dewdrops. Large open garden roses are arranged with sweetheart roses and grasses in a silver ceramic container. They are placed in a tight arrangement, using shades of mauve, burgundy, pink and cream accented with soft greens. This arrangement makes a grand statement in any dining room or formal living room.

{ 19 }

{ Tools & Supplies }

- 2 burgundy morning dew open rose stems with buds
- 2 mauve morning dew open rose stems with buds
- 3 soft pink morning dew open rose stems with buds
- 3 white morning dew open rose stems with buds
- 2 green/mauve single open rose stems
- 3 green/mauve sweetheart rose sprays
- 3 mauve sweetheart rose sprays
- 1 grass bush
- ceramic container with 9" (23cm) diameter
- moss
- silver floral spray paint
- 2 bricks dry floral foam
- 1 floral anchor
- hyacinth sticks
- glue gun
- latex gloves

1. Paint Container

Wearing latex gloves, spray paint the ceramic container silver. Let it dry completely before continuing (about 30 minutes).

2. Trim Foam and Secure

With a glue gun, secure a floral anchor into the inside of the container. Cut one brick of dry floral foam in half, insert it into the container and push it onto the floral anchor to secure. Cut the second brick of foam to 9" (23cm) in length, or the diameter of your container, and insert lengthwise on top of the secured piece of foam. Make sure the two foam bricks fit snugly into the container.

3. Insert Hyacinth Stick

Secure the floral foam by inserting a hyacinth stick through both foam bricks. Trim the excess stick with wire cutters.

5. Add Morning Dew Open Roses

Cut the buds from all of the morning dew open roses to 3" (8cm). Cut all the open rose blooms with a 5" (13cm) stem. Insert the roses and buds randomly in the foam to create a dome-like shape. Insert the stems in farther on the sides than in the center.

4. Add Moss

Cover the floral foam with dampened moss. Tuck the moss in and around the inside of the container, completely covering the floral foam.

6. Add Mauve Sweetheart Rose Sprays

Cut 5" (13cm) mauve sweetheart rose spray stems. Insert them randomly throughout the arrangement.

7. Add Green/Mauve Single Open Roses

Cut two 5" (13cm) green/mauve single open rose stems. Insert them randomly throughout the arrangement.

8. Add Green/Mauve Sweetheart Rose Sprays

Cut three 5" (13cm) green/mauve sweetheart rose sprays. A stem of spray roses should have two roses, one bud and foliage. When inserting the flower stems, consider color placement and separation.

9. Insert Leftover Rose Foliage

Add leftover rose foliage from the cut rose stems. Cut at least a 1" (3cm) stem below where the leaves begin. Insert the foliage randomly throughout the arrangement. The deep green rose leaves will distinguish the roses from each other.

10. Add Grass

Cut four stems of grass clusters from the bush, measuring 10"–18" (25cm–46cm) in length. Insert the taller stems in the top of the arrangement and the shorter ones into the sides at a downward angle.

{ the finished rose garden centerpiece }

magnolia mantle

This elegant piece, designed in a long and narrow brass container, is

perfect for a central spot on your mantle. Use large, impressive

magnolias, with their natural dark green foliage, and blend them with

peonies, dogwood sprays and hanging amaranthus. This piece should

be arranged so that the foliage trails over the mantle for a soft and

natural appearance.

{25}

{ Tools & Supplies }

- 6 beige latex magnolia stems
- 3 beige paper silk peony stems
- 9 soft-colored dogwood sprays
- 2 lavender hanging amaranthus stems
- 2 mauve hanging amaranthus stems
- 3 magnolia foliage stems
- 24" × 4" (61cm × 10cm) brass container
- moss
- sand
- 3 bricks dry floral foam
- 2 floral anchors
- hyacinth sticks
- glue gun

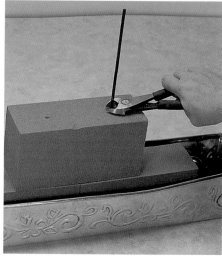

1. Secure Floral Anchors and Add Foam

Using the glue gun, secure two floral anchors by gluing them into the base of the container at each end. Insert two bricks of floral foam onto the floral anchors, end to end, in the center of the container.

2. Add the Final Foam Brick

Center the third brick of floral foam and place it on top of the other two. Insert two hyacinth sticks into the foam to secure the bricks. Trim the excess stick lengths with wire cutters.

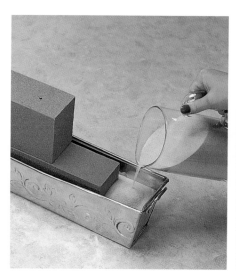

3. Add Sand

Pour sand around the floral foam. Fill the container about two-thirds full. The sand will weigh down the arrangement and make it sturdy. It is very important to weigh a light-weight container down so it will hold the weight of the flowers.

4. Cover With Moss

Cover the foam and sand with damp moss. Tuck any excess moss into the container.

5. Add Peonies

Cut three 4" (10cm) beige paper silk peony stems (measure from the base of the flower head). Insert two of the peonies in the lower front corners of the foam. Insert the third in the top of the foam, slightly right of center, with the flower angled upward.

6. Add Magnolias

Insert one 18" (46cm) beige latex magnolia stem on each end of the container, one 15" (38cm) magnolia stem in the center at the top, one 13" (33cm) magnolia stem in the top-right corner, one 12" (30cm) magnolia stem in the top-left corner and one 19" (48cm) magnolia stem in the center. Bend the 19" (48cm) stem, as well as the side stems, over the edge of the container.

7. Add Dogwood Sprays

Cut five 20" (51cm) dogwood sprays and insert them in the foam randomly on the top and bottom perimeters of the arrangement. Cut four 10" (25cm) dogwood sprays and insert them in the foam throughout the middle part of the arrangement. Bend the stems to flow naturally.

8. Add Amaranthus

Cut two 4" (10cm) mauve and one 4" (10cm) lavender hanging amaranthus stems (measure from the base of the flower to the end of the stem). Cut an 8" (20cm) lavender hanging amaranthus stem. Insert them randomly in the front of the arrangement and off center. Insert some stems at a lower angle and some at a higher angle.

9. Insert Magnolia Foliage

With the leaves and foliage you cut off when adding the magnolias to the arrangement, insert the leaves into the piece, filling in wherever needed.

{ the finished magnolia mantle arrangement }

{ variation }

Try making this arrangement using only one color. This variation incorporates dried materials and features yellow flowers along with deep-colored greenery. The rich combination of sunflowers, magnolias, black-eyed susans, dried amaranthus, ivy, grasses and cattails makes it a perfect autumn arrangement. Notice the structured and segmented design. The flower varieties are each arranged together. However, while it is deliberately arranged, the design is meant to look casual—the flowers appear to be growing naturally out of the container and ivy is cascading down the mantle. Therefore, you can display this arrangement in a formal or casual setting, depending on your preference. Consider displaying this low and wide arrangement on a mantle, bookcase, on a fireplace hearth or on the floor.

tea rose romance

This small arrangement, blooming with Victorian romance, would look beautiful on a bedroom nightstand, in a bathroom or as a simple accent in a sitting room. Choose an elegant silver container that complements the assortment of tea roses and daisies. Pay special attention to the placement of grasses and foliage to achieve that fresh-from-the-garden look.

{ Tools & Supplies }

- 1 lavender miniature tea rose spray
- 1 white miniature tea rose spray
- 1 yellow miniature tea rose spray
- 3 yellow miniature daisy stems with grass
- 1 purple veronica stem
- 1 white astilbe bush
- 1 miniature foliage bush
- 5" (13cm) tall silver container, with a 3" (8cm) diameter

- 1 dry floral foam brick
- 1 floral anchor
- glue gun

1. Trim Floral Foam and Secure

Secure a floral anchor onto the inside bottom of the container with a glue gun. Cut a piece of floral foam 5" (13cm) tall and trim the foam to fit the shape of the container. Push the foam into the container and onto the anchor to secure. The foam should be 1" (3cm) taller than the container.

2. Add the Foliage Bush

Insert the miniature foliage bush stem into the center of the foam and separate the sprigs evenly around the top of the container.

{HELPFUL HINT}

•

When your silver container needs to be cleaned, simply lift the foam and arrangement from the container and reinsert when finished cleaning.

3. Add White Miniature Tea Roses

Cut three sprigs from the tea rose spray measuring 8" (20cm), 6" (15cm) and 5" (13cm). Insert the first two sprigs off-center and insert the third sprig in the front center of the foam. Bend the third sprig over the container edge to give it a loose and flowing appearance.

4. Add Yellow and Lavender Miniature Tea Roses

Cut the yellow and lavender tea rose sprays in various lengths from 7"–8" (18cm–20cm) and insert them randomly throughout the arrangement.

5. Add the Purple Veronica

Cut the veronica into four sprigs in various lengths from 7"–10" (18cm–25cm). Insert them randomly into the foam.

6. Add Yellow Miniature Daisies

Cut three miniature daisy sprigs from each stem in various lengths measuring 8"–14" (20cm–36cm). Measure from the bottom of the stem to the tip of the grass. Insert throughout the arrangement.

7. Add the White Astilbe Bush

Cut all of the sprigs from the astilbe bush. Trim each stem between 4"–9" (10cm–23cm). Fill in the arrangement so the foam is no longer visible.

8. Curl Grass

Use scissors to curl some of the grass sprigs on the miniature daisies to give it a fresh garden look.

{ the finished tea rose romance arrangement }

{variation}

Create this stunning yet simple variation by combining terra-cotta roses and hypericum berries. Featuring large flowers, a compact design and strong color, the result is not as feminine-looking or delicate as the Tea Rose Romance, but instead gives a more masculine look to the same silver container. While it is a small arrangement, it really creates drama. This piece would look lovely on a credenza or an end table for a splash of color in a study. Because of its small size, you could also place the arrangement on a bookcase, amid books and picture frames, or as a decorative accent in just about any room in your home. For a dinner or garden party, make several variations using a range of colors. Line them down the center of the dining table and place votive candles between the arrangements for a very stylish table setting.

spring garden trellis

Bright and colorful buds and flowers welcome the spring season.

Bring the outdoors in with a trellis overflowing with forsythia,

pansies and wisteria, arranged in a whitewash pot. This arrangement

brightens any room and showcases a whimsical yet structured design.

The trick is to feed the forsythia up the trellis as if it had just grown

there. Think of how wonderful this would look on a hearth—or make

a pair for a sideboard or buffet. Coordinate the color

of the flowers to match the décor in any room.

{37}

{ Tools & Supplies }

- 2 purple wisteria stems
- 5 yellow forsythia stems
- 3 medium pansy bushes
- 1 trailing woody stemmed variegated ivy bush, 36" (91cm) long
- 9"–10" (23cm–25cm) diameter whitewash pot
- 30" (76cm) wire topiary form
- moss
- 5" × 18" (13cm × 46cm) green foam cone

- 3 bricks dry floral foam
- 3 floral anchors
- waterproof floral tape
- hyacinth sticks
- glue gun
- craft glue

1. Secure Floral Anchors and Foam

With a glue gun, attach three floral anchors to the base of the container. Cut brick of dry floral foam to 5" (13cm). Insert the foam into the pot and secure it with the floral anchors.

2. Make an Impression of the Pot

With two bricks of foam, place them, one at a time, on the top of the pot. Lightly press to make an impression into the foam so you'll know how much to trim.

3. Trim and Insert Foam

Following the impression, trim the foam to fit the inside of the pot. Insert it into the pot, and then push the foam until it is slightly lower than the top of the pot.

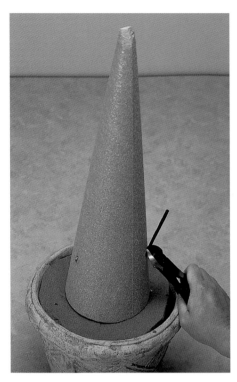

4. Add the Foam Cone

Place the cone on the foam in the pot. Use hyacinth sticks to secure the cone and foam together. Trim any excess stick length.

5. Cover Cone With Moss

Cover the cone with dry moss and secure with craft glue.

6. Add the Wire Topiary Form

Place the wire topiary form over the moss-covered foam cone.

8. Finish Covering the Foam

Add additional moss around the edge of the pot to completely cover the floral foam.

{40}

7. Add More Moss

Stuff the topiary form with more moss to fill in around the cone and form. Do not overstuff the form with moss to allow apace for the flowers.

9. Add the Variegated Ivy

Cut four 34" (86cm) stems from the variegated ivy bush. Start at the top of the topiary form and twist one end of an ivy stem around the top of the wire form to secure. Continue to follow one of the four side wires of the form and cover it with the ivy, twisting around the wire at least four times down to the base of the topiary. Look for any tightly curled vines on the stem and pull them out to make the arrangement look more interesting and natural. Repeat these instructions to cover the remaining three side wires.

11. Attach the Forsythia

Take the longest forsythia sprigs and feed them up the frame of the topiary form. Leave some sprigs loose so they appear to grow naturally up the form.

10. Add the Forsythia

Insert five forsythia stems into the cone, one-third of the way up. The stems should be inserted downward so the forsythia sprigs look as if they are growing up the trellis.

12. Add the Final Forsythia

Insert a 12" (30cm) sprig of forsythia into the moss at the top of the topiary form.

14. Glue Loose Pansy Flowers

Use a glue gun to glue any flowers that have flimsy or fragile stems onto the moss.

13. Add the Pansies

Cut off 2" (5cm) sprigs of pansies from the bush. Insert them randomly throughout the topiary form, into the foam.

15. Add the Wisteria

Cut wisteria sprigs in various lengths from 14"–17" (36cm–43cm). Insert them around the base of the topiary.

16. Insert the Remaining Variegated Ivy

Cut the leftover variegated ivy vines to various lengths from 10"–14" (25cm–36cm) and insert them randomly around the base of the topiary. Finish the arrangement by filling in any holes with moss.

{ the finished spring garden trellis }

springtime vase

This soft springtime flower mix arranged in a tall, thick crystal vase

will enhance any entryway or living room décor. The soft colors,

along with the delicate flower petals, make this arrangement a

lovely piece to use in early spring, when flowers are just beginning to

bud and bloom. The arrangement is so natural looking and abundant

that everyone will ask if it's real. The compound added

to the bottom of the vase gives the illusion of water

in this permanent arrangement.

{ Tools & Supplies }

- 5 large soft pink peony stems
- four 39" (99cm) white delphinium stems
- 5 soft pink lilac stems
- 7 woody or viburnum stems (also called snowballs)
- five 36" (91cm) soft pink cherry blossom stems
- 5 dogwood sprays
- two 45" (1.1m) pussywillow stems
- 13" (33cm) tall crystal vase with 3½" (9cm) diameter opening
- additional vase with 3½" (9cm) diameter opening

- two 12-ounce (336g) boxes of clear floral arranging compound
- long-handled spoon for mixing floral compound
- 1 large pitcher
- latex gloves
- lazy susan trivet (optional)

{HELPFUL HINT}

•

This project is easier to do if you arrange it first in a separate, similar vase and then carefully transfer it to your vase filled with the clear floral compound. The clear compound gives the appearance that the flowers are in water, but be very careful not to slosh the compound, leaving an uneven water line. If leaves or petals fall into it they will be difficult to remove.

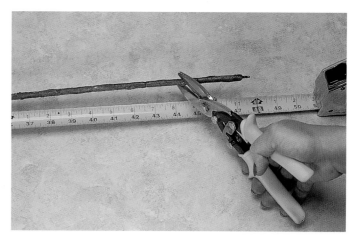

1. Prepare Stems

Trim the pussywillow (from tip to tallest stem) to 45" (1.1m). Next, measure the white delphinium (from tip to tip) to 39" (99cm). Trim the cherry blossom (from tip to tip) to 36" (91cm). Then, measure and snip the peony stems to 24" (61cm), the viburnum to 32" (81cm), the lilac to 23" (58cm) and the dogwood to 24" (61cm). Use heavier wire cutters for large, woody stems. Keep in mind that your shortest stems should be almost twice the height of the vase.

2. Dip Stems in Clear Floral Compound

While wearing latex gloves, prepare the clear floral compound in a large pitcher according to the manufacturer's directions. Dip all of the flower stems into the compound and set them aside to dry for an hour. Woody stems are more porous than plastic stems and are more likely to bleed color into the clear compound. You may want to dip your woody stems twice.

3. Fill Vase with Compound

Before starting, make certain the vase is completely clean inside and out. Pour the clear compound from your mixing container into the glass vase you want to use. Immediately clean off any drips on the inside or outside of the vase. Set the vase aside.

4. Add the White Delphinium

In a separate vase, begin working on your arrangement. Place the white delphinium in the vase. You may want to sit your vase on a lazy susan trivet so you do not have to pick up the vase while arranging the sides and back.

{ HELPFUL HINT }

•

The smaller the diameter of the vase opening, the less floral product you need and the easier it is to hold the shape of the arrangement.

5. Add the Cherry Blossom

Insert the 36" (91cm) cherry blossoms into the vase among the delphinium. Let the stems crisscross each other inside the vase. Don't be concerned about arranging the stems perfectly; they can be adjusted as you go.

6. Add Peonies

Insert the peonies with the buds pulled to the outside to give a natural and flowing appearance.

7. Add Lilacs

Insert the lilac around the outside and allow the flowers to hang over the edge of the vase.

8. Add the Viburnum

Open and spread the branches on each viburnum stem and insert them randomly through the arrangement. Place some stems toward the middle and some near the outside edge among the existing flowers. Allow the viburnum to hang loosely over the outside edge of the vase.

9. Add the Dogwood

Open the dogwood branches and place one stem in the center and insert the remaining stems into the sides. Rotate the vase to view the placement from all sides.

10. Add the Pussywillow

Randomly insert the pussywillow into the center of your arrangement.

11. Gather the Arrangement

Gather the stems into your hand, keeping the arrangement aligned.

12. Transfer Arrangement

With the arrangement gathered in your hand, transfer it into the vase containing clear floral compound. Be careful when inserting the stems so that leaves or petals do not fall into the compound. Do not lift the vase because that will cause the compound to move around. You want a level water line.

13. Make Final Adjustments

Slightly bend some of the stems so they trail over the side of the vase. Let the vase sit undisturbed for 48 hours and keep it away from extreme temperatures. Do not pull stems in and out of the vase or slosh the compound. The compound will harden, creating a permanent arrangement.

❀
{ the finished springtime vase }

❀
{ variation }

With the versatility of a glass vase, you can alter the flowers in the Springtime Vase to create a completely different look. While it is seasonally appropriate to use softer pinks, creams and greens in the springtime, you may want to add drama and bolder colors in the winter months. Add red tones to give a warm glow to winter and holiday arrangements and feature hearty blooms. Try this winter variation using red gladiolas, red roses, white magnolias and white branches. Gladiolas are excellent flowers for arranging because of their stiff petals and height, creating stately drama and elegance in a dining room or front entryway. The magnolias soften the arrangement and add fullness, the roses add intense color and the white branches open up the arrangement, making it light and airy. Use this for a New Year's or holiday party or display it all winter long. Because this variation is very linear, it would also match a décor with contemporary or Eastern influences.

The arrangements in this section can be characterized as loose, unstructured, just-plucked and natural, as if you had gone for a walk, picked some flowers and placed them in water. The arrangements are simple and casually arranged. The flowers featured in these

field garden

projects are organized in a number of ways. Some are grouped by color and texture; others are arranged with similar flowers from the same family; and others are grouped with flower varieties that grow and behave in a similar way.

section 2

popular field garden flowers:

BEGONIA · BLACK-EYED SUSAN · COSMOS · DAISY · GERANIUM · HYDRANGEA · LIATRIS · LILAC
LISIANTHUS · PANSY · PEONY · QUEEN ANNE'S LACE · SWEET PEA · VERONICA · YARROW

summer geranium basket

This colorful arrangement is large and welcoming, and would be lovely placed by a door or a fireplace in the summer. You could also use it as a cheerful centerpiece for a family gathering. It is a festive way to celebrate summertime, with vibrantly-colored flowers and foliage. The whitewashed basket, filled with trailing ivy and garden geraniums, is lightly accented with corkscrew willow branches.

{55}

{ Tools & Supplies }

- 1 red trailing ivy geranium bush
- 2 large red geranium bushes
- 1 large pink geranium bush
- 4 small cream geranium bushes with red edges
- 1 geranium foliage bush
- 2 corkscrew willow stems
- 20" (50cm) whitewash fireside basket with handle
- two 9" × 12" (23cm × 30cm) sheets of green foam
- eight 12" (30cm) green chenille stems
- moss
- hyacinth sticks
- masking tape

1. Cut and Secure Foam

Cut two pieces of green foam to fit in the bottom of the basket. For this basket, the foam pieces measure 9" × 12" (23cm × 30cm). Secure the foam pieces together by inserting two hyacinth sticks into both foam pieces on each end. Cut off the excess stick lengths.

2. Insert Chenille Stems

Twist four 12" (30cm) chenille stems together and lay them horizontally over the foam. Repeat this technique vertically. Insert the chenille stems through the bottom of the basket and draw the foam snug with the bottom of the basket.

NOTE: Do not pull the chenille stems too tightly or you will slice through the foam.

3. Secure the Chenille Stems

Pull and twist the chenille stems together under the basket and trim the ends. Put masking tape over the ends of the chenille stems to cover the sharp ends.

4. Cover With Moss

Cover the foam and the inside of the basket with moss.

5. Add the Trailing Ivy Geranium Bush

Separate the stems and open the foliage on the ivy geranium bush. Insert the stem in the back center of the foam under the handle. Arrange the geraniums throughout the foliage.

6. Add the Cream Geraniums

Insert two cream geranium bushes on each side of the basket handle and toward the front of the arrangement.

7. Add the Pink Geraniums

Cut all but five pink geraniums from the bush. Trim them close to the bottom of the bush to keep long stems. Insert the geranium bush into the foam, slightly behind center. Bend some of the stems under the handle so the geraniums are on both sides of the handle.

8. Add the Pink Geranium Stems

Insert the individual pink geranium stems randomly throughout the arrangement.

9. Add the Red Geranium Bush

Cut all but three red geraniums from one of the geranium bushes. Insert the red geranium bush stem in front of the pink geraniums, on the opposite side of the handle.

10. Add the Remaining Red Geraniums

From the second red geranium bush, cut all but three flowers. Insert the stem of the bush in the center and in front of the pink geraniums. Insert all of the individual red geranium stems randomly throughout the arrangement.

11. Add the Geranium Foliage

Cut 10" (25cm) foliage sprigs from the geranium foliage bush. Insert these throughout the arrangement, filling in where necessary. Insert some stems through the front of the basket to give a more natural appearance. Fill in any holes in the back.

12. Add Corkscrew Willow

Insert the two stems of corkscrew willow at the top, off-center, and on opposite sides of the handle.

{ the finished summer geranium basket }

garden mosaic

You'll love the freedom this versatile arrangement gives you. Don't worry about a specific form. It should look as though you just picked the flowers from your garden, so give it a natural look. Its abundance of color will liven up any room and add a lighthearted touch to any décor. While the colors provide a vibrancy to this arrangement, there are only three varieties of flowers, all similar in style and behavior. Use a stunning silver container to create a timeless finish to this stylish piece.

{61}

{ Tools & Supplies }

- 3 large hot pink peony stems with buds
- 1 frosted lavender sweet pea stem with vine
- 1 frosted yellow sweet pea stem with vine
- 2 stems each of yellow, mauve and white cosmos
- 1 stem each of dark pink, gold, yellow-red, pink, light yellow, and orange ranunculus
- 6" (15cm) square aluminum container
- 1 dry floral foam brick
- floral anchor
- glue gun

1. Secure Floral Anchor and Foam

Glue the floral anchor into the bottom of the container. Cut the foam to fit the container. The foam should measure 1" (3cm) taller than the container.

2. Add the Peonies

Cut the peony buds and set them aside. Cut the three large peonies to 4" (10cm) stems lengths. Insert two of the peonies into the top of the foam, slightly off center. Insert the third peony into the side of the foam. To create a dramatic effect, insert the stems at staggering heights.

3. Add the Peony Buds

Insert the buds, with 6" (15cm) stems, in the opposite lower corners of the container —one in one corner and two in the opposite. Bend the stems downward.

4. Add the Foliage

Cut the leftover peony foliage with stem lengths varying from 1"–2" (3cm–5cm). Insert the foliage randomly throughout the arrangement.

5. Add the Ranunculus

Cut the ranunculus stems to 7" (18cm) and insert them throughout the arrangement in same-color clusters. Insert some stems in deeper than others to give more dimension.

6. Add the Cosmos

Cut sprigs of cosmos in all colors, with stems in various lengths from 7"–8" (18cm–20cm), and insert them throughout the arrangement.

{ the finished garden mosaic arrangement }

7. Add the Sweet Peas and Foliage

Cut sprigs of sweet peas to various lengths between 1"–2" (3cm–5cm) and set aside. Cut foliage the same length. Insert the sprigs of foliage throughout the arrangement and fill in where needed to cover the exposed foam. Then insert the sweet peas randomly.

provincial pair

Relax and unwind in a room with these matching arrangements,

inspired by French country style. A front entryway would be ideal for

a pair of these tall arrangements. They are one-sided arrangements in

tall, decorative tin containers, filled with lush field flowers. This

inviting floral design, in shades of blues and purples, accents the elegant

forms of the delphinium, lilac and hydrangea. The

colors and flowers offer a soothing, calming feeling

to the room, while the height gives it drama.

{ Tools & Supplies }*

- 1 tall blue delphinium stem
- 1 tall purple delphinium stem
- 2 single blue hydrangea stems
- 1 open lavender hydrangea stem
- 3 hand-wrapped plum poppy stems
- 2 multicolored pansy bushes
- 4 tall purple liatris stems
- 2 purple lilac stems
- 1 bunch dried white flowering birch branches
- 1 blue lilac stem
- 1 small variegated ivy bush
- moss
- floral foam
- hyacinth stick
- sand
- 15" (38cm) tall decorative tin container with a 7" (18cm) diameter opening

Supplies listed are needed to make one arrangement.

1. Add Sand

Fill the container with sand, about halfway full. This will weigh the arrangement down and prevent it from falling over.

2. Trim the Foam

Cut two bricks of foam to fit snugly into the top of the container. The foam should measure 1" (3cm) below the top of the container.

3. Insert and Secure the Foam

Insert the trimmed bricks of foam into the container and secure them with a hyacinth stick. Trim any excess.

4. Cover With Moss

Fill in the open spaces with scrap pieces of foam and then cover with damp moss. This will add greater stability when arranging.

5. Add Flowering Birch Branches

Insert the birch in the back of the container, from side to side. The branches should be at least one and a half times the height of the container. For this arrangement, the branches measure 36" (92cm) from the top of the container to the tip of the branches.

6. Add the Delphinium

In front of the birch branches, insert a stem of blue and purple delphinium side-by-side, measuring about 33" (84cm) from the top edge of the container to the tip of the delphinium.

{HELPFUL HINT}

•

The measurements given in this project measure from the top of the pot to the tip of the stem. Because it is such a tall container, add at least 5" (13cm) to each stem to sufficiently secure the stems into the foam. For example, the birch branches need to be at least 41" (104cm) tall.

7. Add the Liatris

Insert the four purple liatris in front of the delphinium. The two middle liatris measure 22" (56cm) from the top edge of the container to the tip of the liatris; the two outside liatris measure 20" (51cm).

8. Add the Hydrangea

Insert one open lavender hydrangea in front of the liatris and in the middle of the arrangement, measuring 18" (46cm) from the top edge of the container to the top of the flower. Insert two single blue hydrangea on either side of the open lavender hydrangea, measuring 15" (38cm) from the top edge of the container.

9. Add the Lilacs

Insert one blue lilac in front of the hydrangea and in the center of the arrangement. It should measure 13" (33cm) from the top edge of the container to the tip of the stem. Insert two purple lilacs on either side of the blue one. Bend the outside stems of the lilacs to slightly hang over the container to give a more natural and relaxed look.

10. Add the Variegated Ivy Bush

Insert the ivy bush stem into the front center of the arrangement, below the lilac.

11. Add the Plum Poppies

Cut one 10" (25cm) stem of plum poppies and two 6" (15cm) stems. Cut the buds from the poppy stems to measure 7" (18cm) in length. Insert the poppies at staggered heights in the front center, and insert the buds randomly among the poppies. Bend some of the poppy stems and buds to trail over the edge of the container. To finish, bend the trailing ivy over the container and among the poppies.

{ the finished provincial pair }

{ variation }

For a dramatic change to this arrangement, alter the colors of the flowers. This variation was designed with open roses, dendrobian orchids, baby tears, liatris, allium and flowering branches. The structure of the arrangement is also different from the very balanced and symmetrical Provincial Pair. This variation is very linear, from the upper right to the lower left. There is a waterfall effect of orchids and greenery growing out of the left side of the arrangement. The stiff and sturdy liatris are fanned out, creating drama and contrast among the roses, baby tears and orchids. This arrangement looks stunning against a dark wall, on a pedestal or in front of a mirror.

PROVINCIAL PAIR

{69}

pot of poppies

This quick and easy arrangement features tall poppies in yellow and

orange, perfect for any patio or deck. The beauty in this arrangement

comes from its simplicity. The radiant poppies provide a burst of

color as well as a unique shape. The clay pot used for this project

was spray painted and textured for a more natural look and

interesting texture.

{71}

{ Tools & Supplies }

- 4 tall yellow poppy stems
- 6 tall orange poppy stems
- 6" (15cm) clay pot
- moss
- moss green spray paint
- 1 brick dry floral foam
- 2 floral anchors
- hyacinth stick

- glue gun
- spray bottle with water
- latex gloves

1. Paint the Pot

Wearing latex gloves, lightly spray the 6" (15cm) clay pot with moss green spray paint.

2. Spray Pot With Water

Spray water on the clay pot. Do not let it dry before next step.

3. Paint Pot Again

Spray the wet clay pot again with paint. This gives the pot a textured look. Let the pot dry before you begin working on the arrangement.

4. Secure Anchors and Add Foam

Glue two floral anchors into the bottom of the pot. Cut ⅓ off a foam brick. Stack the two pieces of the foam on top of each other and insert the brick into the pot.

5. Secure the Foam

Insert a hyacinth stick into both pieces of the foam, off center, and cut off the excess length.

6. Add the Moss

Completely cover the foam with moss and tuck the excess inside the pot.

7. Add the Tallest Poppies

Cut five 28" (71cm) poppy stems and insert them randomly in the foam. Mix the four yellow blooms and six orange blooms. To enhance the natural look, take a stem with a bud attached and curl the stem around a pencil. When the pencil is removed, pull out the curled stem slightly.

8. Add the Shorter Poppies

Cut four 18" (46cm) poppy stems and insert them around the pot's perimeter. This will make your arrangement more of a centerpiece, to be viewed on all sides. For a balanced piece, be sure to evenly distribute the different colored poppies.

{ HELPFUL HINT }

•

If you would like to create a taller arrangement, cut all of the stems to 28" (71cm). Poppies are known for their winding yet sturdy stems.

❀

{ the finished pot of poppies }

❀

{ variation }

Change this arrangement slightly by altering poppies for cosmos and assorted grasses, creating a loose and airy arrangement. The grasses expand the arrangement and give it a casual, whimsical look. The container also contributes to the style of the arrangement. You can leave it as a regular terra cotta pot or give it texture by painting it, spraying it with water and painting it again. You may also sponge-paint the pot to give it a textured look. Whatever container you decide to use, be sure that it complements the simplicity of the arrangement. For a little extra drama, create this variation along with other versions and display them together. Each pot should hold a cluster of one flower variety at various heights. Create pots of tulips, hyacinths, peonies, gerbera daisies, alstroemeria and sunflowers. Display the grouping in a greenhouse window, window box, on a patio, or even on a kitchen windowsill.

summertime pitcher

Take a relaxing weekend hour to make this joyful summertime

arrangement of field flowers that look carefree in a simple ceramic

water pitcher. Quick and easy to make, this arrangement would be

a great accent in your kitchen or on your enclosed porch or patio.

Use sweet black-eyed susans with dainty waxflower and veronica to

create an arrangement that is whimsical, spirited

and inviting.

{77}

{ Tools & Supplies }

- 5 yellow black-eyed susan stems
- 4 white black-eyed susan stems
- 3 lavender waxflower stems
- 3 green veronica stems
- green ceramic pitcher
- 1 dry floral foam brick
- floral anchor
- glue gun

1. Secure Floral Foam

Glue a floral anchor into the bottom of the pitcher. Cut the foam to fit snugly into the pitcher. The foam does not need to come to the pitcher edge. It is better if it rests lower.

2. Add Yellow Black-Eyed Susans

Cut three 10" (25cm) stems of yellow black-eyed susans and insert them in the lower perimeter. Cut one 14" (36cm) stem and insert it into the foam, off-center. Cut one 18" (46cm) stem and insert in the center. Bend the stems slightly for a natural look.

3. Add White Black-Eyed Susans

Cut four stems of white black-eyed susans in various lengths from 15"–18" (38cm–46cm). Insert them throughout the arrangement.

5. Add the Veronica

Cut three 16" (41cm) stems of veronica. Insert them deeply throughout the arrangement.

4. Add the Waxflower

Cut three stems of waxflower to various lengths from 16"–18" (41cm–46cm). Insert them randomly throughout the arrangement. This adds a burst of color to the arrangement.

{ the finished summertime pitcher }

Bulb gardens are simplistic in design. Most flower varieties are planted in well-defined sections. Bulb flowers, such as tulips, amaryllis, iris and daffodils, grow naturally with more than one bloom on each stem, so it is common to see bulb

beautiful bulb garden

flowers in clusters in landscape design. Combine bulb arrangements with grasses to give them a fresh and vibrant look. Look for silk counterparts with wired stems that can be shaped to look like you picked them right out of your own beautiful bulb garden!

section 3

popular bulb flowers:

ALLIUM · AMARYLLIS · CROCUS · CYCLAMEN · DAFFODIL · DAHLIA · EREMURUS · GLADIOLA
HYACINTH · IRIS · LILY · NARCISSUS · PAPERWHITE · SCILLA · TULIP

{ P R O J E C T   E L E V E N }

blooming window box

What better way to welcome springtime into your home than with a

window box filled with flowering bulb plants! Can you can feel the

breezes blowing in your kitchen window over these colorful clusters?

A rustic wood crate, spotted with moss, is the key ingredient to this

arrangement. Whether you choose a large, dramatic crate or a small,

charming box, fill it to the brim with the colors of spring.

{ Tools & Supplies }

- 7 lavender iris stems
- 1 purple violet bush
- 4 yellow daffodil bushes
- 5 orange tulip stems
- 3 yellow foxglove stems, at least 38" (97cm) tall
- 7 red gerbera daisy stems
- 1 pink variegated azalea bush
- 2 white daisy clusters
- 9¼" x 12" x 18" (24cm x 30cm x 46cm) wooden crate

- moss
- wood tone paint
- 10 dry floral foam bricks
- 9 floral anchors
- hyacinth sticks
- glue gun

1. Remove Boards From Crate

Tip the crate on its side. Using a hammer, remove the top two boards from one side of the crate.

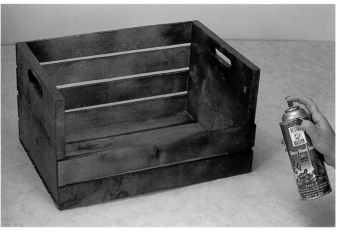

2. Paint the Crate

Paint the entire crate using wood tone paint on both sides. Let it dry.

3. Secure the Floral Anchors

Glue nine floral anchors into the bottom of the crate.

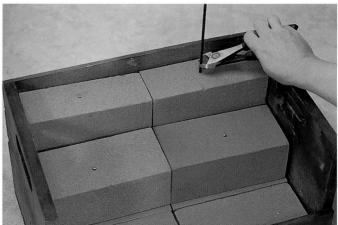

4. Add the Floral Foam

Begin in the back of the crate and insert two bricks of foam on their sides. Stack two more on top of these. Then insert four more bricks of foam, flat and in front of the others. This creates a tiered effect with the foam. Finally, insert two more bricks side by side and lying flat. Secure the bricks together with hyacinth sticks and cut off the excess stick lengths.

5. Add the Moss

Cover the foam with moss. Using a glue gun, conceal the space between the front boards with moss.

6. Add the Yellow Foxglove

Cut 38" (97cm) yellow foxglove stems (measuring from tip to tip). Insert them in the upper left-hand corner, third row, of the foam. Push the stems in at different heights, so they measure 35" (89cm), 35" (89cm) and 30" (76cm) out of the foam.

7. Add the Azalea and Violet Bushes

Cut the azalea and violet bushes with 3" (8cm) stems on each. Insert the bushes deep into the foam in the front row, with the violet bush on the left and the azalea bush on the right.

8. Add White Daisy Clusters

Cut two 14" (36cm) stems of the daisy clusters. Insert both stems in the front row, between the azaleas and violets.

9. Add the Lavender Iris

Cut the irises into the following lengths: three 21" (53cm) stems, two 18" (46cm) stems and two 15" (38cm) stems. Insert the irises in the middle row, on the left, as a cluster. Insert the taller stems in the center of the cluster and the shorter ones around the perimeter. Bend the stems slightly over the crate.

10. Add Gerbera Daisies

Cut two 17" (43cm) stems of gerbera daisies, three 15" (38cm) stems and two 10" (25cm) stems. Insert them to the right of the irises, in the center of the middle row. Arrange them in a cluster.

12. Add the Orange Tulips

Insert three 28" (71cm) tulips and one 24" (61cm) tulip randomly across the third row. Insert one 22" (56cm) in the middle row, tulip right of center.

11. Add the Daffodil Bushes

Cut two 22" (56cm) daffodil bushes and two 16" (41cm) bushes. Insert them in the center of the top row, with the taller daffodils in back and the shorter ones in the front. Spread the flower stems apart for an airy appearance.

{ the finished blooming window box }

hanging hyacinth basket

This hanging willow pocket basket is filled with an assortment of miniature grape hyacinths. These flowers give a lovely burst of color to the early spring season. Growing out of the hanging basket, this arrangement would look beautiful on a veranda or on a door. You may want to hang it in your kitchen or powder room because of its delicate touch as a welcoming reminder of spring.

{89}

{ Tools & Supplies }

- 2 stems each of miniature grape hyacinth in purple, blue, green and green/mauve
- 3 coral miniature grape hyacinth stems
- 1 button leaf trailing vine bush
- 1 maidenhair ivy bush
- willow pocket basket with an 8" (20cm) opening
- moss
- 2" (5cm) wide sheet of green foam
- glue gun

1. Secure the Foam and Add Moss

Line the front part of the basket with damp moss so the foam will not show through the basket. Using a glue gun, secure a piece of 5" × 5" × 2" (13cm × 13cm × 5cm) foam into the basket. Be sure to put the glue on the inside of the basket and let it cool off for a few seconds before inserting the foam (otherwise the foam will melt). Cover the foam with moss and tuck any excess into the basket.

2. Add the Grape Hyacinth

Cut one stem of each hyacinth color (there are five total) 10"–12" (25cm–30cm) in length. Insert these stems toward the back of the arrangement. Put the tallest in the center and fan the stems from left to right. Curl the leaves with your hands to give the foliage a natural look. For a tighter-looking arrangement, simply insert the stems deeper into the foam.

3. Add the Shorter Grape Hyacinth

With the remaining hyacinths, trim the stems to approximately 5"–6" (13cm–15cm) long. Insert them in front of the taller ones randomly throughout the basket opening. Bend some of the stems over the basket's edge to give the flowers a natural look.

4. Add the Grape Hyacinth Foliage

Cut leftover foliage from the hyacinth with 2" (5cm) stems and insert it randomly throughout the arrangement.

5. Add the Maidenhair Foliage

Cut twelve to eighteen sprigs of maidenhair ivy from the bush, each with about 2" (5cm) stems. The number of stems used depends on the desired fullness. Be sure to insert some stems into the back of the arrangement to give it depth.

6. Prepare the Button Leaf Vine

Open up the button leaf vine and spread its branches. Cut the stem into two or three sprigs. Note that only the sprig's stem will be sturdy enough to go into the foam.

7. Add Final Touches

Insert the button leaf vine into the arrangement and spread out the vines so they trail over the basket edge. If you have trouble securing the buttonleaf, use floral picks. You may want to add some damp moss trailing over the basket edge or tucked within the willow of the basket. Also, moss can be hot glued to the outside of the basket.

✿

{ the finished hanging hyacinth basket }

✿

{ variation }

Alter the flowers and the colors used in the hanging basket to create the perfect accent for the winter months. Use ranunculus, holly berries, grasses and maidenhair fern. As the featured flower, ranunculus has a strong texture and a deep, vibrant color. The colors in the flowers, berries and greenery are deep and lush, giving it a bold and sturdy appearance that you would expect to find in the wintertime. When decorating for the holidays, anchor this piece to the wall with a piece of festive ribbon. After the holidays, change the ribbon and keep it up for the rest of the season. Hang this arrangement in the kitchen or on a door. It is a welcoming sight, no matter what the season!

simply modern lilies

While lilies are a timeless flower, this arrangement creates a modern

twist blending them with allium in a blue glass vase filled with marbles.

The flowers and foliage are arranged in a very angular manner and the

flower colors are deliberately complementary. The result is a dramatic

and contemporary arrangement, which will make a strong statement

in any room in your house. Use it as a centerpiece or

on an end table.

{95}

{ Tools & Supplies }

- 3 rubrum lily stems
- 3 green allium stems
- 3 corkscrew willow stems
- 2 grass bushes
- 12" (30cm) tall square blue crystal vase
- two 1 pound (448g) bags of 14mm blue decorative marbles

1. Add the Marbles and Allium

Add one bag of the marbles to the vase. Cut three stems of allium measuring 17" (43cm), 24" (61cm) and 26" (66cm). Place them in the vase, allowing the tallest stem to fall to the back-left side. The middle stem should be placed on the right side of the vase, and the shortest stem should be in the front-left corner. The vase is square and the front of the arrangement is a corner, not a flat side of the vase.

2. Add Rubrum Lilies

Cut two 18" (46cm) stems of rubrum lilies and one 23" (58cm) stem. Insert both into the front-center of the arrangement. Do not be concerned with positioning your stems perfectly for now. More marbles will be added near the end of this project to secure everything in place.

3. Add Grass Bushes

Cut the grass bushes to 22" (56cm) and 26" (66cm) in length. Insert the taller stem in the left side of the vase. Insert the shorter stem in the right side. Allow some of the grasses to hang over the edge of the vase.

4. Add the Corkscrew Willow

Cut three stems of corkscrew willow that measure 24" (61cm), 28" (71cm) and 32" (81cm). Insert the longest stem on the left side. Insert the 28" (71cm) stem off to the right side, and the shortest stem in the front-center.

5. Add Decorative Marbles

Gather the arrangement in your hand and carefully pour the remaining marbles in the vase. You may need to adjust the arrangement if the marbles shift the stems.

6. Curl the Grasses

Using scissors, curl some of the grasses to give a natural and interesting touch to your arrangement.

{ the finished simply modern lilies arrangement }

tulips *and* narcissus

A perfect touch to any windowsill or shelf, this charming arrangement combines white tulips and narcissus in a subtle ceramic container. Minimal in color and design, this project is beautiful with its notable flower varieties and its simplicity. Tall stems give this piece height, while the grasses give the piece more substance and depth, allowing it to stand on its own on a dresser or end table.

{ Tools & Supplies }

- 3 cream or green tulip stems
- 5 miniature narcissus or white daffodils
- 2 bunches of ¼" (6mm) wide bladed grass, 13"–14" (33cm–35cm) in length
- natural ceramic container, 7½" x 5" x 4½" (19cm x 13cm x 11cm)
- moss
- 2 dry floral foam bricks
- 2 floral anchors
- 1 hyacinth stick
- glue gun

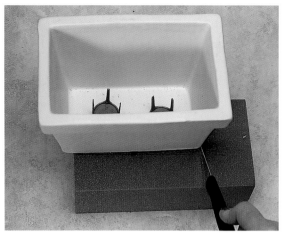

1. Secure Floral Anchors and Trim Foam

Glue two floral anchors into the container base. Mold and cut the foam to the dimensions of the container. The foam should be $\frac{3}{4}$" (2cm) lower than the top of the container. For this container, two bricks of foam were cut to the following measurements: $5\frac{1}{2}$" x $2\frac{1}{2}$" x 1" (14cm x 6cm x 3cm) and $6\frac{1}{4}$" x $2\frac{1}{2}$" x 2" (16cm x 6cm x 5cm).

2. Insert the Foam

Insert the foam into the container, with the smaller piece pushed into the floral anchors.

3. Insert the Hyacinth Stick

Connect and secure the two pieces of foam with a hyacinth stick. Cut the excess.

4. Add Moss

Cover the foam with damp moss and tuck the excess moss inside the container.

5. Add the Wide Bladed Grass

Cut off each blade of grass from the bush, then cut each blade in half and at a steep angle so it has a natural look. The grasses should be about 13"(33cm) tall. Insert each blade into the foam at staggered heights and completely cover the top surface. Bend a few of the blades to give a natural look.

{simple **variations**}

The beauty of this arrangement is its simplicity. The delicate narcissus flowers complement the heartier tulips and coordinate because they are both white. The white contrasts with the vibrant green leaves and grass to give the arrangement balance and fullness.

You may want to try variations of this arrangement. Keep it simple— try all one variety, such as different colored tulips. You may also want to create an arrangement that uses one color and a few different flowers. Keep one common trait throughout the arrangement to maintain an overall mood and theme.

7. Curl the Grasses

Curl the narcissus grasses with scissors. This will give the arrangement a natural and airy feel.

6. Add the Narcissus

Cut five 2" (5cm) stems of narcissus (measured from the base of the greens). Add them randomly in the container.

8. Prepare the Tulips

Push the tulip leaves toward the flower head. Cut three 12" (30cm) tulip stems.

{HELPFUL HINT}

•

Make sure that you bend and arrange the stems of these flowers so they look natural.

9. Add the Tulips

Insert the tulips across the center of the arrangement, with the center tulip slightly lower than the other two.

{ the finished tulips and narcissus }

A fruit and vegetable arrangement creates an inviting display in a kitchen or dining room. There are many fruits and vegetables that are so lifelike, they are often mistaken for the real thing. When choosing the fruits and vegetables, remember to

• fruit & vegetable garden •

use compatible types with realistic colors and sizes. You may also want to enhance the look of a vegetable or fruit arrangement with berries and foliage as well as vines and stems. Remember that floral picks are often necessary when arranging fruits and vegetables to secure them in floral foam.

section 4

popular garden fruits & vegetables :

APPLE · ARTICHOKE · ASPARAGUS · BANANA PEPPER · CABBAGE · CARROT · CHILI PEPPER · GRAPE

KUMQUAT · LEMON · LOGANBERRY · PEACH · PEAR · PLUM · RASPBERRY

berry wreath

This is a simple arrangement to construct, but it is a beautiful addition to any room. Use a twig wreath and arrange assorted berries and vines throughout in deep jewel colors. Display this wreath anytime from late summer all the way through the fall and winter months. Hang it from a door or use it as a wall accent piece. The more sporadic the berries appear, the better, giving a natural, rustic feel.

{ Tools & Supplies }

- 5 raspberry vine stems with foliage
- 5 red and purple raspberry stems
- 3 loganberry stems
- 14" (36cm) twig wreath
- 30"–36" (76cm–91cm) of 1" (3cm)wide wired, sheer, plum ribbon
- glue gun

1. Attach the Ribbon

To make a hanger for the wreath, take a 30" (76cm) piece of the wired sheer plum ribbon and tie it loosely in a knot around the wreath. To tie a bow with the ribbon, cut the ribbon to 36" (91cm).

2. Trim the Ribbon Ends

Fold the ribbon ends in half and cut them at a slant.

3. Add Raspberry Vines With Foliage

Cut five raspberry vines with 2" (5cm) stems. Insert them into the wreath all the way around. Using the glue gun, secure the vines and leaves as you go with a touch of glue.

4. Add the Loganberry

Cut four sprigs from each stem of loganberry. Allow 2" (5cm) stems for each sprig. Insert them throughout the wreath and secure with glue. It is better to add the glue to the stem before inserting it into the wreath.

5. Add Red and Purple Raspberries

Cut five stems of red and purple raspberries in half. Allow for 2" (5cm) stems on each sprig. Insert these stems randomly throughout the wreath. Fill in on the sides of the wreath as well. Bend the stems so the berries stick out of the foliage for a wild look.

❀

{ the finished berry wreath }

mexican pepper swag

Give your kitchen a little zing with this swag of peppers and zinnias.

Red and orange raffia, used to tie the pepper and flower bundles, add

to the fiesta of colors. The raffia-braided swag is virtually hidden

behind the bright red chili pepper clusters and the larger banana pep-

per clusters. The colors in this unique arrangement will enhance your

décor and bring a little excitement to your kitchen!

{ 111 }

{ Tools & Supplies }

- 4 clusters of large chili peppers
- 3 red, 3 yellow and 3 green banana peppers
- 1 orange zinnia stem
- 2 yellow zinnia stems
- 24" (61cm) long braided natural raffia swag
- 1 package red raffia
- 1 package orange raffia
- 1 package 20-gauge florist wire

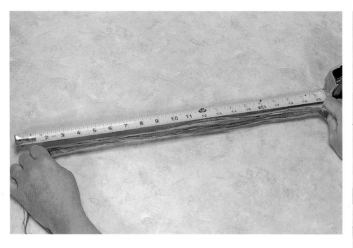

1. Prepare the Raffia

Measure and cut the red and orange raffia to 20" (51cm) lengths.

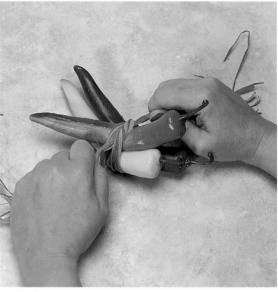

2. Make Banana Pepper Clusters

Wrap three banana peppers together, one each in red, green and yellow. Tie them with five to eight strands each of red and orange raffia. Wrap the raffia three times around the stems and tie it in a double knot to secure. Make three clusters.

3. Trim the Raffia Ends

Trim the raffia ends with scissors to your desired length.

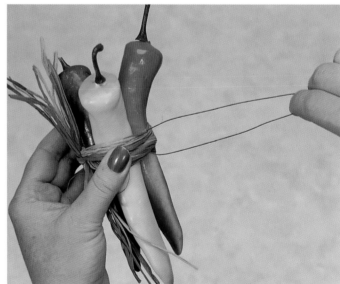

4. Attach Wire to Banana Pepper Clusters

Insert one 20-gauge florist wire through each cluster of banana peppers, bend in half, twist to secure and set aside.

5. Make Chili Pepper Clusters

Wrap five to eight strands each of red and orange raffia around the wire stems of a cluster of chili peppers. Wrap them twice and tie in a double knot to secure. Make four clusters.

6. Trim the Raffia

Cut 4"–5" (10cm–13cm) raffia ends.

7. Bend Chili Pepper Wires

Bend over the clusters of wires on the chili peppers and hide them within the peppers. The wires will be more hidden when attached to the swag.

8. Attach Wire to the Chili Peppers

Insert a 20-gauge florist wire through each chili pepper cluster, bend in half, twist to secure and set aside.

9. Make the Zinnia Cluster

Cut two yellow zinnias and one orange zinnia, leaving about a 4"–5" (10cm–13cm) stem with leaves on each. Tightly wrap the zinnias together with florist wire.

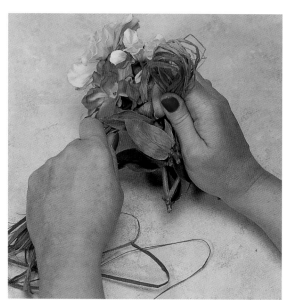

10. Tie the Zinnia Clusters

Cut 30" (76cm) lengths of red and orange raffia. Wrap the raffia around the zinnia bundle and hide the wire. Tie a large bow with five to eight strands of each color.

11. Attach the Zinnia Clusters

Attach the bundles to the swag with wire. Trim any excess wire with wire cutters.

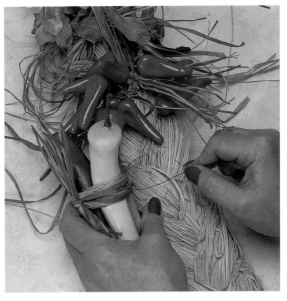

12. Attach Chili Peppers

Attach the four clusters of chili peppers to the swag. Thread the wire under the raffia and secure.

13. Attach Banana Peppers

Attach three bundles of banana peppers to the swag. Try to cover up as much of the swag as possible.

{ the finished mexican pepper swag }

fruit bowl centerpiece

This classic fruit bowl arrangement never goes out of style. Choose whatever fruits most appeal to you and suit your décor. I've used an abundant selection of apples, pears, plums, grapes, kumquats and fruit vines, arranged in a tin compote. Proudly display your arrangement as a centerpiece on your dining table or on the buffet. This piece works both for a formal occasion and for everyday use.

{117}

{Tools & Supplies}

- 3 red apples
- 3 green apples
- 7 assorted bunches of grapes
- 2 kumquats
- 4 fruit vine stems
- 5 pears
- 3 plums
- 12" (30cm) diameter pounded tin compote
- ¼" (6mm) green waterproof floral tape
- moss
- sand
- 3 bricks dry floral foam
- 1 floral anchor
- hyacinth sticks
- floral picks
- glue gun
- lighter fluid (optional)

1. Insert Floral Anchor and Foam

Glue a floral anchor into the bottom of the container. Trim one brick of foam 4½" (11cm) long and secure it on the floral anchor. To add weight to your container, pour sand into the base and around the foam, if necessary.

2. Fill the Container With Foam

Add scraps of foam to fill in the container base. Insert two 6" (15cm) bricks of floral foam on top of the first brick.

3. Secure the Foam

Insert two hyacinth sticks through each brick of foam to secure. Trim any excess stick length.

4. Tape Foam in Place

Clean the container surface with lighter fluid to remove any oils or residue so the tape adheres. Cross the container with ¼" (6mm) waterproof floral tape over the foam and secure it to the sides of the container.

5. Add Moss

Completely cover the foam with damp moss. On the sides, insert the moss under the tape first and then cover the surface.

6. Attach the Floral Pick to the Grape Clusters

Thread a wire on a floral pick through the top stem of all of the grape clusters. Pull the stem securely to the floral pick with the attached wire and twist tightly.

7. Insert Four Grape Clusters

Insert the clusters into the foam. The grapes should fall over the sides of the container.

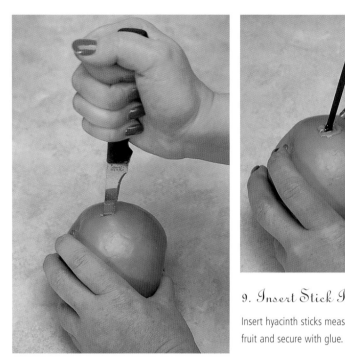

9. Insert Stick Into Fruit

Insert hyacinth sticks measuring about 2" (5cm) in length into the fruit and secure with glue.

8. Prepare the Fruit

Use a paring knife to make a small hole in the fruit. Randomly make your holes in a different part of each piece of fruit for a more interesting arrangement.

10. Add Two Apples and a Pear

Insert one green apple, one red apple and a green pear into the center of the arrangement.

11. Prepare Kumquats and Plums

Wire a floral pick to each kumquat and plum. You may also use other medium-sized fruits.

12. Add Kumquats and Plums

Insert the kumquats and plums deeper into the foam and slightly off-center around the two apples and pear.

13. Insert Additional Apples and Pears

Trim the hyacinth sticks of the remaining apples and pears to 2" (5cm) in length. Randomly insert and fill in the lower part of the arrangement. The closer the fruit is to the edge, the deeper you should insert it into the foam.

15. Add the Remaining Clusters of Grapes

Fill in any bare spots with the remaining clusters of grapes.

14. Add the Top Grapes

Insert a cluster of grapes into the center top of the arrangement. Let the grapes hang over the apples and pears.

16. Add Fruit Vines

Insert four stems of fruit vines off center and randomly into the arrangement. Two vines should be 13" (33cm) long and two should be 9" (23cm) long. Insert them high enough to allow the vines to hang naturally.

17. Finish With Additional Moss

Once all the fruit is inserted where you like it, lift up the trailing grapes at the sides of the container and add more moss for a bountiful appearance. Fill in holes throughout the arrangement with damp moss.

{ the finished fruit bowl centerpiece }

In addition to the mail-order and online resources listed here, check your local craft and floral supply shops for general floral tools and supplies. Purchase fine silk flowers from local craft stores or directly from your florist.

{**domestic** resources}

C.M. OFFRAY & SON, INC.
360 Route 24
Chester, NJ 07930
(800) 551-LION
www.offray.com
• *Decorative ribbons*

DESIGN MASTER COLOR TOOL INC.
P.O. Box 601
Boulder, CO 80306
(303) 443-5214
www.dmcolor.com
• *Floral color sprays, paints and tints*

DICK BLICK ART MATERIALS
P.O. Box 1267
Galesburg, IL 61402-1267
(800) 828-4548
fax (800) 621-8293
www.dickblick.com
• *Wire cutters, ribbon, raffia, glue and general art supplies*

FLORACRAFT
One Longfellow Place
P.O. Box 400
Ludington, MI 49431
(616) 845-0240
www.floracraft.com
• *Floral sheet foam and general floral supplies*

FLORIST DIRECTORY
www.eflorist.com
• *Web directory to assist in finding a florist in your area*

MARIEMONT FLORIST, INC.
7257 Wooster Pike
Cincinnati, OH 45227
(800) 437-3567
www.mariemontflorist.com
• *Contact author, general information and assistance*

SAVE-ON-CRAFTS
16601 N. 25th Ave. Suite 101
Phoenix, AZ 85023
(602) 993-3364
fax (602) 993-3285
www.save-on-crafts.com
• *Floral wires, foam, adhesives, tapes, raffia, moss,*
silk flowers, greenery, ivy garlands and topiary forms

SILK FLOWERS EXPRESS
3467 Rutrough Rd.
Roanoke, VA 24014
www.silkflowersexpress.com

SOCIETY OF AMERICAN FLORISTS
1601 Duke St.
Alexandria, VA 22314
(800) 336-4743
www.safnow.org
• *General information about the floral industry*

W.J. COWEE, INC.
28 Taylor Ave.
P.O. Box 248
Berlin, NY 12022
(800) 658-2233
www.cowee.com
• *Wooden floral picks and general floral supplies*

WINWARD SILKS
For local distributor, call (800) 888-8898
or e-mail wsilks@winwardsilks.com
www.winwardsilks.com
• *International importer and distributor of*
fine-quality silk flowers

{international resources}

FLORAL ART MALL
21/262 Centerway Road
Orewa
New Zealand
www.floralartmall.com
+64 9427 5681
• *Retailer of fresh and silk flowers,*
florist supplies and books

Create gorgeous gifts and decorations with silk and dried flowers!

Make your holidays brighter and more special by creating your very own floral décor! Cele Kahle shows you how to create a variety of gorgeous arrangements, swags, topiaries, wreaths and even bows. There are 19 creative projects in all, using silk foliage, berries, fruit and ribbon. Each one comes with materials lists, step-by-step guidelines and beautiful full-color photos.

ISBN 1-58180-259-5, paperback, 128 pages, #32124-K

Capture the essence of the seasons with these simple, stunning floral arrangements. With a few basic techniques, a handful of materials, and a little creativity, you can make eye-pleasing accents for every room in your home. You'll find all the flower arranging advice you need inside, along with 15 projects using silk flowers, greenery, leaves, pinecones, gourds and more.

ISBN 1-58180-108-4, paperback, 96 pages, #31810-K

Whether you're planning a grand Thanksgiving dinner, a tropical theme party, or a romantic dinner for two, you'll find a wealth of creative silk and dried floral projects inside—each one designed to make your special occasions stand out. Terry L. Rye makes creating centerpieces easy, affordable and fun. The results are simply magnificent!

ISBN 1-55870-598-8, paperback, 128 pages, #70537-K

Here are 20 beautiful wreath projects, perfect for brightening up a doorway or celebrating a special time of year. You'll find a range of sizes and styles, utilizing a variety of creative materials, including dried herbs, sea shells, cinnamon sticks, silk flowers, Autumn leaves, Christmas candy and more. Clear, step-by-step instructions ensure beautiful, long lasting results every time!

ISBN 1-58180-239-0, paperback, 144 pages, #32015-K

These books and other fine North Light craft titles are available from your local art & craft retailer, bookstore, online supplier or by calling 1-800-448-0915.